SIMPLY CONVECTION OVEN COOKBOOK FOR BEGINNERS

Quick and Easy Convection Oven Recipes for All the Family | From Breakfast to Dessert

Kathleen Nolove

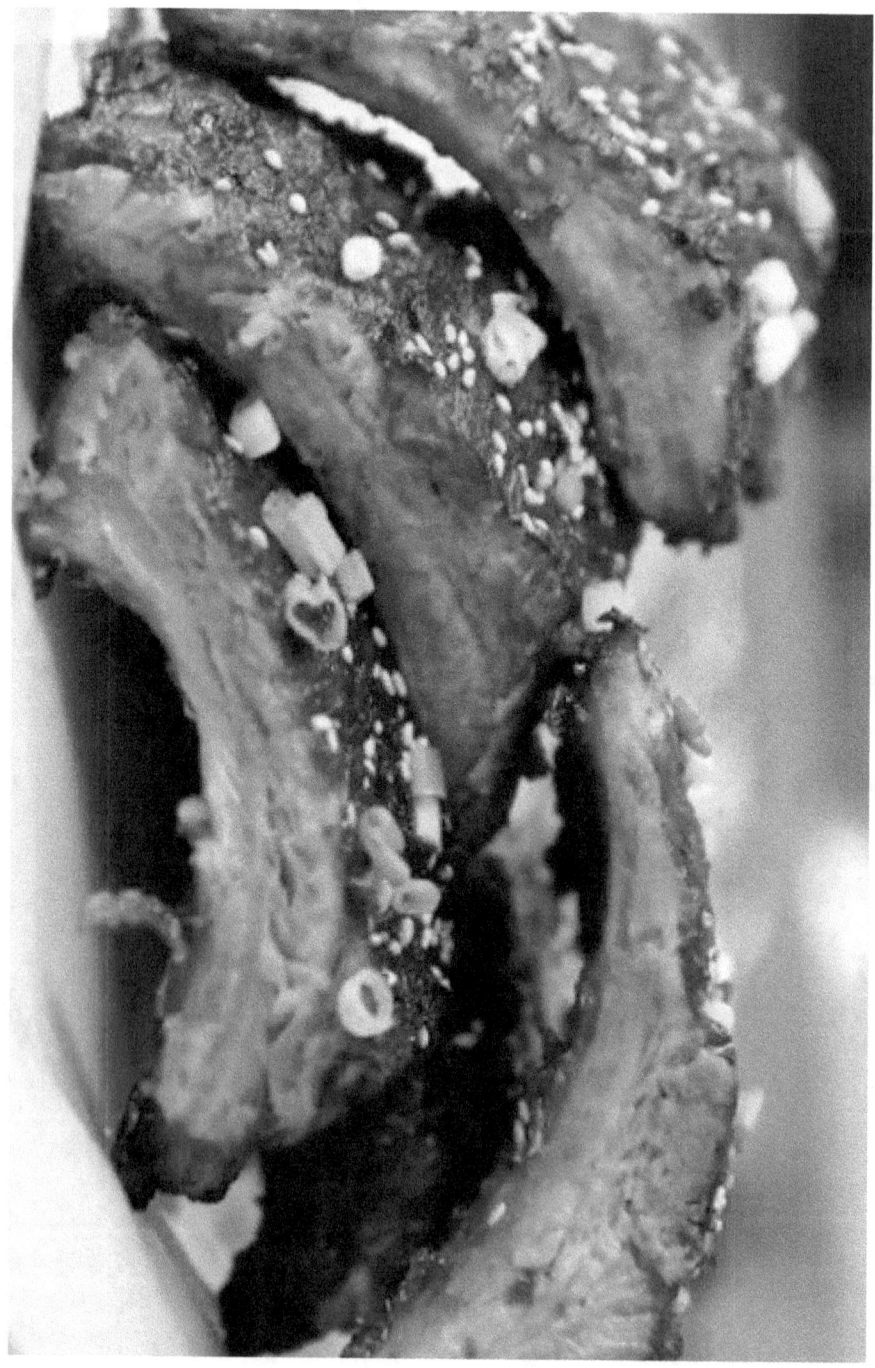

© Copyright 2021 by _____Kathleen Nolove_____ - All rights reserved.

The following Book is reproduced below with the goal of providing information that is as accurate and reliable as possible. Regardless, purchasing this Book can be seen as consent to the fact that both the publisher and the author of this book are in no way experts on the topics discussed within and that any recommendations or suggestions that are made herein are for entertainment purposes only. Professionals should be consulted as needed prior to undertaking any of the action endorsed herein.

This declaration is deemed fair and valid by both the American Bar Association and the Committee of Publishers Association and is legally binding throughout the United States.

Furthermore, the transmission, duplication, or reproduction of any of the following work including specific information will be considered an illegal act irrespective of if it is done electronically or in print. This extends to creating a secondary or tertiary copy of the work or a recorded copy and is only allowed with the express written consent from the Publisher. All additional right reserved.

The information in the following pages is broadly considered a truthful and accurate account of facts and as such, any inattention, use, or misuse of the information in question by the reader will render any resulting actions solely under their purview. There are no scenarios in which the publisher or the original author of this work can be in any fashion deemed liable for any hardship or damages that may befall them after undertaking information described herein.

Additionally, the information in the following pages is intended only for informational purposes and should thus be thought of as universal. As befitting its nature, it is presented without assurance regarding its prolonged validity or interim quality. Trademarks that are mentioned are done without written consent and can in no way be considered an endorsement from the trademark holder.

Table of Content

INTRODUCTION 7

BREAKFAST 11
- Bacon, Egg, and Cheese Breakfast Hash 12
- Southwestern Hash With Eggs 14
- Maple-Glazed Sausages and Figs 16
- Asparagus and Leek Quiche with Gruyere 18
- Holiday Brunch Casserole (Grits Casserole) 20
- Watching Over the Bay Sunday Brunch Benedict 21
- Easy Oven Frittata 22

APPETIZERS & SNACKS 25
- Mozzarella Sticks 26
- Baked French Fries 28
- Fried Pickles 30
- Smoky Potato Chips 32

VEGETABLES 35
- Ratatouille Casserole 36
- Tofu 38
- Thai Roasted Vegetables 40
- Tortellini Primavera 42
- Sweet Potato Casserole 44
- Delicious Roasted Garlic Mushrooms 46

SEA FOODS 47
- Lemon Pepper Dill Fish 48
- Healthy Fish and Chips 50
- Quick Paella 52
- Coconut Shrimp 53
- Ingredient Catfish 55
- Cilantro-Lime Fried Shrimp 56
- Bang Panko Breaded Fried Shrimp 58

POULTRY 61
- Korean Chicken Wings 62
- Almond Flour Coco-Milk Battered Chicken 64
- Basil-Garlic Breaded Chicken Bake 65
- Buffalo Chicken Wings 67
- Honey and Wine Chicken Breasts 69

BBQ Chicken Recipe From Greece 71
Lemon-Pepper Chicken Wings 73
Caesar Marinated Grilled Chicken 75
Crispy Southern Fried Chicken 77

MEAT 79

Steak With Garlic-Herb Butter 80
Steak Bites With Mushrooms 82
Korean Beef BBQ 84
Roast Beef 86

BREAD 89

Cheddar Jalapeno Cornbread 90
Family Banana Nut Bread 92
Basic Fruit Bread 94
Mini Pizza With Italian Sausage 95
Roasted Garlic Pizza With Garlic Sauce 97

CAKE & DESSERT 99

Cinnamon Apple Tart 100
Blackberry Peach Cobbler 102
Blueberry Cream Cheese Croissant Puff 104
Oatmeal Cookie Peach Cobbler 105
Oatmeal Raisin Cookies 107
Peanut Butter and Jelly Bars 109
Peanut Butter Cookies 111
Cinnamon Pear Oatmeal Crisp 113

MEASUREMENT CONVERSION CHART 114

INTRODUCTION

Have you heard of an oven? This heating mechanism is a great alternative to the traditional heaters, especially for your kitchen. Convection ovens are smaller compared to the conventional ones. This is because their air movement technology has lessened the need for large ceiling areas. Unlike the conventional ones, these are specially designed with a fan that circulates the air inside it. This mode of heating is the most efficient one that has been developed to date. This can be considered a much better option than the conventional ovens. You must have heard the term 'low calorie', however, ovens do not have low-calorie features but they do manage to consume less amount of power.

Convection ovens cook almost six times faster than the normal stoves, and not only does it reduce the cooking time, it also enhances the flavors of the food. These ovens though small, are technically advanced. The technology used in ovens is the same one that is used on commercial airplanes to heat them. The convection heating system's efficiency is highly dependent on the recipes used by the user. Of course, the user has complete control over the level of heating and the features of the oven. The specialty of an oven is that it starts cooking the food from the top and the bottom surfaces and not just the top. This gives not only the extra flavors but also prevents the disasters like the burning of food as it keeps the food evenly warmed. This is another great advantage of an oven. However, it is important to correctly follow the instructions given when purchasing these ovens. Convection ovens are great for people who wish to cook in bulk. This depends on the user's characteristics. Small households may cook on a regular basis, but someone who is fond of baking cookies or enjoying baking bread will require an oven. This type of oven is also suited for people who wish to use it for heating green stuff, for instance, for the use of a steamer. Another great advantage of this oven is that it can be used for cooking a whole meal. If the oven is of good quality, the dish can be cooked perfectly well and does not have the starchy taste or the burnt taste that is common with traditionally cooked food. The cooking process on this oven is much faster than other ceramic or traditional stoves. You should also note that this is significantly more energy efficient as it does not require more energy consumption than other types of stoves.

The oven is best suited for those people who feel that they would like to cook in huge batches of food. The choice of an oven depends on the intended use of the oven. You should choose the right oven for a particular purpose. Another advantage of the oven is that it makes the food come out perfectly by nourishing the food with liquid. This in no way requires you to thaw the frozen food in the traditional oven if you have frozen food for your oven. Of course, you should not cook frozen food on a normal heating device as it may turn hazardous.

In order to have the best out of your oven, you should follow the instructions to a T for safety measures. Before you purchase the convection oven, ensure that it is of a good quality. Ensure that the oven heats evenly. Also, ensure that it operates without making too much noise. It should also be very convenient for storage of the food. It should also be easy to clean.

Different Types of Convection Oven

There are several types of Convection Ovens; the most common types are divided into two categories. The first type is differentiated by the placement of the fan and additional heating element; this is the regular and the true convection oven.

The second type is classified by its placement or position in the kitchen; the major types are the countertop convection ovens and the floor models.

Regular convection oven

A regular convection oven is a device used to heat various types of food and beverages. A convection oven possesses several 'products' for delivering heat to the food placed in the oven.

True convection oven

A true convection oven is a natural method of cooking that is used in most restaurants. The cost of running a true convection oven is virtually nothing because they cut out the expensive internal electric or gas-powered convection fan, called a blower, which costs over $400 to replace. The idea behind the true convection oven is to use the air patterns that are naturally produced during cooking to distribute heat evenly to all areas of the oven.

Countertop convection oven

A countertop convection oven is like a countertop microwave. Instead of microwaves, it sends the hot air around and cooks the food from convection. And it has a door for the steam to get out.

Floor model convection oven

A floor model convection oven is a thing to envy. It's large enough to hold a 13"x9" cake tin, or the 8"x8" pan I use to bake brownies. The convection fan hubbub its blades mounted at the top of the dome-shaped door to mix the warm air as it cooks your meal.

It's a solid iron machine that makes my brownies with a crackling sound.

Breakfast

Bacon, Egg, and Cheese Breakfast Hash

Preparation time: 15 minutes

Cooking time: 20 minutes

Servings: 4

INGREDIENTS:

- 2 slices bacon
- 4 tiny potatoes
- 1/4 tomato
- 1 egg
- 1/4 cup shredded cheese

DIRECTIONS:

1. Preheat the oven to 200°C or 400°F on bake mode. Set bits of bacon on a double-layer tin foil.

2. Cut the vegetables to put over the bacon. Crack an egg over it.

3. Shape the tin foil into a bowl and cook it in the oven at 177°C or 350°F for 15-20 minutes. Put some shredded cheese on top.

NUTRITION:
- Calories: 150.5
- Carbs: 18g
- Protein: 6g
- Fat: 6g

Southwestern Hash With Eggs

Preparation time: 55 minutes

Cooking time: 15 minutes

Servings: 4

INGREDIENTS:

- 1-1/2 lbs. pork steak
- 1 teaspoon vegetable oil
- 1 large potato, peeled and cubed
- 1 medium-sized onion, chopped
- 1 garlic clove, minced
- 1/2 cup green pepper, chopped
- 1 can diced tomatoes and green chilies
- 1 beef bouillon cube
- 1/2 teaspoon ground cumin
- 1/2 teaspoon salt
- 1/4 teaspoon pepper
- 1/8 teaspoon cayenne pepper
- 4 eggs
- 3/4 cup shredded cheddar cheese
- 4 corn tortillas (six inches)

DIRECTIONS:

1. Cook pork in oil until brown and add potato, onion, garlic, green pepper. Cook for 4 minutes.

2. Stir in tomatoes, bouillon, cumin, salt, pepper, and cayenne. Cook with low heat until potatoes become tender.

3. Create four wells inside the hash and crack eggs into them.

4. Bake it in the oven uncovered for 10-12 minutes at 177°C or 350°F and scatter some cheese over it.

5. Serve over tortillas.

NUTRITION:
- Calories: 520
- Carbs: 29g
- Protein: 49g
- Fat: 23g

Maple-Glazed Sausages and Figs

Preparation time: 20 minute

Cooking time: 20 minutes

Servings: 2

INGREDIENTS:

- 2 tablespoon maple syrup
- 2 tablespoon balsamic vinegar
- 2 packages (12 ounces each) fully cooked chicken, cooked garlic sausages
- 8 fully ripe fresh figs, cut lengthwise
- 1/2 large sweet onion, minced
- 1-1/2 lbs. Swiss chard, with sliced stems, minced leaves
- 2 teaspoon olive oil
- Salt and pepper

DIRECTIONS:

1. Preheat the oven to 232°C or 450°F, mix syrup with 1 tablespoon vinegar in a tiny bowl. Put sausages with figs on a one-layer foil-lined oven tray.

2. Roast for 8-10 minutes by grazing the syrup mix throughout the cooking.

3. Cook the onions in the oven in a bowl with plastic wrap for 9 minutes.

4. Mix oil and seasoning with 1 teaspoon of vinegar. Serve the chards with figs and sausages.

NUTRITION:

- Calories: 450
- Carbs: 42g

- Protein: 34g
- Fat: 17g

Asparagus and Leek Quiche with Gruyere

Preparation time: 35 minutes

Cooking time: 30 minutes

Servings: 4

INGREDIENTS:

- 9-inch tart shell
- 1/2 lb. asparagus, minced into 1/2-inch pieces
- 1 little leek, around 2-3 ounces, with white and light green parts
- 1/2 cup whole milk and 1/2 cup heavy cream
- 4 big eggs
- 1/2 cup minced Gruyère

DIRECTIONS:

1. Whisk milk and heavy cream with eggs in a medium mixing bowl.

2. Put asparagus and leek evenly in the shell. Glug the cream mixture on top and sprinkle minced cheese evenly over it.

3. Preheat the oven at 177°C or 350°F for 25 minutes before placing the quiche inside.

4. After the custard sets completely, broil for 3-5 minutes to make it brown.

NUTRITION:

- Calories: 194
- Carbs: 9g
- Protein: 5g
- Fat: 15g

Holiday Brunch Casserole (Grits Casserole)

Preparation time: 10 minutes

Cooking time: 50 minutes

Servings: 4

INGREDIENTS:

- 4 cups water
- 1 cup grits
- 1/2 tablespoon salt & paprika
- 1 lb. sausage
- 1/2 cup margarine
- 1/4 lbs. garlic cheese (put 1 tablespoon garlic on white cheese)
- 1/2 cup milk
- 3 eggs

DIRECTIONS:

1. Preheat the oven at 190°C or 375°F.

2. Fry and drain the sausage. Cook the grits in boiling salted water for 5 minutes.

3. Stir margarine and cheese until it melts before adding milk, eggs, and sausages, and mixing them properly. Pour it inside an 11 -3/4 x 9-3/8 x 1-1/2 " aluminum pan.

4. Bake the mixture at 177°C or 350°F for 30-45 minutes.

5. Spread paprika over the casserole and cover it with foil.

NUTRITION:

- Calories: 403.2
- Carbs: 16.8g
- Protein: 16.5g.

Watching Over the Bay Sunday Brunch Benedict

Preparation time: 10 minute

Cooking time: 10 minutes

Servings: 4

INGREDIENTS:

- 4 Bays English Muffins cut and toasted
- 4 eggs
- 1 lb. Pancetta, chopped
- Smoky paprika
- Fresh cilantro
- Hollandaise sauce

DIRECTIONS:

1. Put a muffin in the oven on both sides of the plates.
2. Make crisp pancetta in a small pan, cook eggs over easy, and prepare hollandaise sauce on the side.
3. Put pancetta evenly on top of muffins, and eggs over easy above the pancetta.
4. Put hollandaise sauce on top and sprinkle smoky paprika and freshly minced cilantro.

NUTRITION:

- Calories: 560
- Carbs: 39g
- Protein: 43g
- Fat: 29g.

Easy Oven Frittata

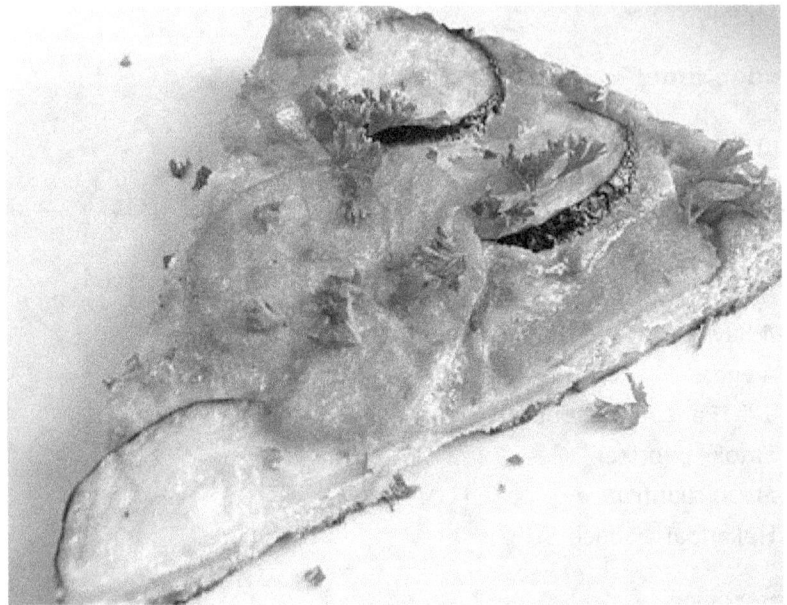

Preparation time: 15 minutes

Cooking time: 35 minutes

Servings: 6

INGREDIENTS:

- 8 eggs
- 1 onion minced
- 1 clove garlic diced
- 1 cup vegetables
- 1 cup sausage or bacon minced
- 1 cup cheese shredded & 1 teaspoon Parmesan cheese
- 1 cup milk
- 1 tablespoon flour
- Butter
- Salt and Pepper

DIRECTIONS:

1. Preheat the oven to 232°C or 450°F. Sauté onions in a pan to soften them.
2. Cook garlic and any vegetables with meat.
3. Whisk the eggs with milk, flour, and cheese. Put them inside a buttered pan, cook for twenty minutes. Sprinkle salt and pepper on top.

NUTRITION:
- Calories: 129
- Carbs: 2.8g
- Fat: 9.6g.

Appetizers & Snacks

Mozzarella Sticks

Preparation time: 5 minutes

Cooking time: 6 minutes

Servings: 4

INGREDIENTS:

- 1 cup all-purpose flour
- 1 cup seasoned breadcrumbs
- 1 teaspoon baking soda
- 1/2 cup marinara sauce
- 1 tablespoon milk
- 2 eggs
- 8 sticks of mozzarella cheese, each about 1-ounce

DIRECTIONS:

1. Turn on the oven, set the temperature to 400 degrees F, and then select the oven cooking method.
2. Meanwhile, place flour in a shallow dish and then stir in baking soda until mixed.
3. Crack the eggs in a bowl, add milk and then whisk until blended.
4. Take a separate shallow dish and then spread panko breadcrumbs in it.
5. Working on one cheese stick at a time, dredge in flour mixture, coat in egg mixture, dip in the egg mixture, and then coat in breadcrumbs.
6. Arrange the cheese sticks in the oven basket, spray with oil, and then cook for 6 minutes.
7. Serve the cheese sticks with the marinara sauce.

NUTRITION:

- Calories: 440
- Fat: 22g
- Carbs: 40g
- Protein: 19g
- Fiber: 2g

Baked French Fries

Preparation time: 10 minutes

Cooking time: 25 minutes

Servings: 4

INGREDIENTS:

- 4 medium potatoes, each about 8-ounce
- 1 teaspoon salt
- 1/2 teaspoon ground black pepper
- 1/4 cup and 1 teaspoon olive oil

DIRECTIONS:

1. Turn on the oven, set the temperature to 475 degrees F, and then select the oven cooking method.//
2. Meanwhile, scrub the potatoes and then cut each potato into 12 wedges.

3. Transfer the potato wedges into a large bowl, cover with hot water and then soak potatoes for 10 minutes.

4. Line the baking pan with a parchment sheet, drizzle with 1/4 cup oil, and then sprinkle with 1/2 teaspoon salt and 1/4 teaspoon ground black pepper.

5. After 10 minutes, drain the potatoes, pat dry with paper towels, and then toss with 1 teaspoon oil until evenly coated.

6. Spread the potato wedges on the prepared baking pan, cover with foil and then bake for 5 minutes.

7. Uncover the pan, and then continue baking the potato wedges for 15 minutes until the underside of the wedges turns golden brown.

8. Flip the potato wedges, spread them in an even layer, and then continue to bake them for 10 minutes until evenly brown on all sides.

9. Serve straight away.

NUTRITION:
- Calories: 83
- Fat: 3.5g
- Carbs: 12g
- Protein: 1.5g
- Fiber: 1.5g

Fried Pickles

Preparation time: 5 minutes

Cooking time: 20 minutes

Servings: 32

INGREDIENTS:

- 32 slices of dill pickles
- 1/2 cup all-purpose flour
- 1/2 teaspoon garlic powder
- 1/2 teaspoon salt
- 1/2 teaspoon cayenne pepper
- 2 cups panko breadcrumbs
- 2 tablespoons chopped dill
- 2 tablespoons dill pickle juice
- 3 eggs

DIRECTIONS:

1. Turn on the oven, set the temperature to 400 degrees F, and then select the oven cooking method.

2. Meanwhile, place flour in a medium bowl, and then stir in salt.

3. Crack the eggs in a medium bowl, add garlic powder, cayenne pepper, and pickle juice and then whisk until combined.

4. Place panko breadcrumbs in a shallow dish, add dill and then stir until combined.

5. Working on one slice of dill pickle, dredge it in flour mixture, dip into the egg mixture, coat in crumb mixture, and place in the oven basket.

6. Spray oil over the pickle slices and then cook for 7 to 10 minutes per side until crisp and golden.

7. Serve straight away.

NUTRITION:

- Calories: 26
- Fat: 1g
- Carbs: 1g
- Protein: 1g
- Fiber: 0g

Smoky Potato Chips

Preparation time: 5 minutes

Cooking time: 20 minutes

Servings: 6

INGREDIENTS:

- 1 1/2 pound potatoes
- 3/4 teaspoon salt, divided
- 1/4 teaspoon ground black pepper
- 1 tablespoon smoked paprika
- 2 tablespoons olive oil

DIRECTIONS:

1. Turn on the oven, set the temperature to 400 degrees F, and then select the oven cooking method.

2. Meanwhile, slice the potatoes into round, about 1/8-inch thick, and then pat dry with paper towels.

3. Take a large bowl, place the potato slices into the bowl, add 1/2 teaspoon salt, paprika, oil, and black pepper and then toss until coated.

4. Spread the potato rounds in the single layer on the baking pan and then bake for 20 minutes until nicely browned.

5. When done, sprinkle salt over the potato chips, cool completely, and then serve.

NUTRITION:
- Calories: 130
- Fat: 4.7g
- Carbs: 20g
- Protein: 2g
- Fiber: 2g

Vegetables

Ratatouille Casserole

Preparation time: 10 minutes

Cooking time: 15 minutes

Servings: 8

INGREDIENTS:

For the veggies

- 2 eggplants
- 6 Roma tomatoes
- 2 yellow squashes
- 2 zucchinis

For the sauce

- 2 tablespoons olive oil
- 1 onion, diced
- 4 cloves garlic, minced
- 1 red bell pepper, diced
- 1 yellow bell pepper, diced
- Salt, to taste
- Pepper, to taste
- 28 oz. can of crushed tomatoes (795g)
- 2 tablespoons chopped fresh basil, from 8-10 leaves

For the herb seasoning

- 2 tablespoons chopped fresh basil, from 8-10 leaves
- 1 teaspoon garlic, minced
- 2 tablespoons chopped fresh parsley
- 2 teaspoons fresh thyme
- Salt, to taste
- Pepper, to taste
- 4 tablespoons olive oil

DIRECTIONS:

1. Preheat the oven to 375F (190 C).
2. Cut the eggplant, tomatoes, squash, and zucchini into roughly 1/16-inch (1-mm) round, and keep them aside.
3. Make the sauce: Heat the olive oil in a 12-inch (30-cm) oven-safe dish over medium-high warmth. Sauté the onion, garlic, and bell chilies until soft, around 10 mins.
4. Season with salt and chilies; at that point, add the squashed tomatoes. Mix until the ingredient is completely joined.

Eliminate from heat, then add the basil. Mix again, and point smooth the top of the sauce with a spatula.
5. Organize the cut veggies in rotating designs, (for instance, eggplant, tomato, squash, zucchini) on top of the sauce from the external edge to the center of the container.
6. Season with salt and chilies.
7. Make the herb seasoning: In a little bowl, combine the basil, garlic, parsley, thyme, salt, chilies, and olive oil. Spoon the herb seasoning over the vegetables.
8. Cover the dish with foil and bake for 40 mins. Remove the foil cover and heat for an additional 20 mins, until the vegetables are soft.

NUTRITION:

- Calories: 268;
- Fat: 5.1g;
- Carbs: 43g;
- Protein: 13.7g

Tofu

Preparation time: 10 minutes

Cooking time: 15 minutes

Servings: 8

INGREDIENTS:

For the Tofu:
- 2 8oz Blocks Extra Firm Tofu (450g)
- 1 tablespoon sesame Oil
- For the Kung Pao Sauce:
- 1 tablespoon Rice Vinegar
- 2 tablespoons Soy Sauce
- 1 tablespoon Hoisin Sauce
- 1 tablespoon Maple Syrup
- 1 Tsp. Cornstarch

For the Veggies:
- 1 tablespoon Sesame Oil
- 5 Dried Red Chilies
- 1 teaspoon Crushed Garlic
- 1 teaspoon Minced Ginger

- 1 Red Pepper
- 3 Spring Onions (about 1/3 cup chopped)
- 1/4 cup (37g) Roasted Salted Peanuts

For Serving:
- Basmati Rice or Cauliflower Rice
- Chopped Spring Onions

DIRECTIONS:

1. Press the tofu for 20 mins. Either utilize a tofu press or spot the tofu on a plate, with another plate on top of it and afterward place something substantial on top, similar to a hefty pot.
2. While the tofu is squeezing slash up the red chilies and spring onions and stir up the sauce ingredient in a bowl.
3. At the point when the tofu is squeezed, cut it into cubes and afterward add to a griddle with the sesame oil and fry, tenderly turning over the tofu until it's pleasantly fried. Eliminate from the container.
4. To the dish, add sesame oil and dried chilies and fry for 2 mins. At that point, add the squashed garlic, ginger, bell chilies, spring onions, and peanuts. Sautéed food for 2 mins.
5. Include the tofu and pour over the sauce and sautéed food until the sauce has thickened.
6. Serve over basmati rice or cauliflower rice finished off with a sprinkle of spring onions.

NUTRITION:

- Calories: 268
- Fat: 5.1g
- Carbs: 43g
- Protein: 13.7g

Thai Roasted Vegetables

Preparation time: 10 minutes

Cooking time: 20 minutes

Servings: 8

INGREDIENTS:

- 2 red onions, cut into wedges
- 2 red capsicums, cut into chunks
- 2 yellow capsicums, cut into chunks
- 2 kumara, peeled, cut into chunks
- 1 eggplant, sliced
- 200ml vegetable broth made with 200ml boiling water and 3 teaspoons broth powder
- Oil spray
- 5 medium tomatoes

Dressing:

- 3 kaffir lime leaves, finely chopped
- 1 red chili, deseeded, diced

- 1 stalk lemongrass, bruised, chopped
- 1 cup fresh coriander
- 2cm-piece fresh ginger, peeled, chopped
- 2 cloves garlic, crushed
- 6 tablespoons oil
- 2 tablespoons salt-reduced soy sauce

DIRECTIONS:

1. Preheat oven to 200°C. Line an enormous simmering tin with greaseproof paper. Add onions, capsicums, kumara, and eggplant. Pour broth over. Shower with oil.
2. Cook vegetables for 45 mins, turning until mellowed and softly burned. Add tomatoes and cook for 15 additional mins.
3. To make the dressing, place all ingredients in a blender and whizz until smooth. Season, then organize vegetables on a serving platter, sprinkle dressing over, and throw delicately to serve.

NUTRITION:

- Calories: 268
- Fat: 5.1g
- Carbs: 43g
- Protein: 13.7g

Tortellini Primavera

Preparation time: 10 minutes

Cooking time: 20 minutes

Servings: 5

INGREDIENTS:

- 1 (14.1 ounces) can 1 14-ounce can vegetable broth or reduced-sodium chicken broth
- 2 tablespoons all-purpose flour
- 1 tablespoon extra-virgin olive oil
- 3 cloves garlic, sliced
- 3/4 cup of shredded Parmesan cheese or a cup of shredded fontina cheese
- 1 tablespoon of fresh tarragon chopped
- 1/8 teaspoon salt
- 16-ounce bag of frozen mixed vegetables or 4 cups of freshly chopped vegetables, such as broccoli, carrots, and snap peas.
- 1 (16 ounces) package 1 16-ounce package frozen cheese tortellini

DIRECTIONS:

1. Place a big pot of water and heat to boil.
2. Then, whisk broth and flour in a little bowl. In a huge pan, heat the oil over medium heat and add garlic and cook, mixing until simply starting to brown, 1 to 2 mins. Add the broth combination to the dish, heat to the point of boiling and cook, blending incidentally, until the sauce is sufficiently thick to cover the rear of a spoon, around 3 mins. Eliminate from the warmth and mix in cheese, tarragon (or dill or chives), and salt.
3. Add vegetables and tortellini to the bubbling water; return the water to a stew and cook until the vegetables and tortellini are delicate, 3 to 5 mins. Add to the dish with the sauce and mix to cover.

NUTRITION:

- Calories: 268
- Fat: 5.1g
- Carbs: 43g
- Protein: 13.7g

Sweet Potato Casserole

Preparation time: 15 minutes

Cooking time: 30 minutes

Servings: 4

INGREDIENTS:

- 2 cup sweet potatoes
- 1/4 cup melted butter
- 1 1/2 tablespoon milk
- 1/4 cup honey
- Vanilla
- 1 large egg
- 1/4 cup brown Sugar
- 1/4 cup wheat flour

- 2 tablespoon butter
- 1/2 cup chopped pecans
- Cooking spray

DIRECTIONS:

1. Spray baking sheet with cooking spray.
2. In a large mixing bowl, combine milk, honey, sweet potatoes, vanilla, melted butter, and egg. Mix well.
3. In another mixing bowl, combine brown sugar and flour. Cut in 3 tablespoons butter till crumbly. Add pecans and mix well.
4. Sprinkle the mixture over sweet potatoes.
5. Place on 1-inch rack and cook for 25-30 minutes at 350 C (High) or until golden brown.
6. Serve Immediately.

NUTRITION:

- Calories: 310
- Total Fat: 13g
- Carbs: 49g
- Protein: 3g

Delicious Roasted Garlic Mushrooms

Preparation time: 10 minutes

Cooking time: 25 minutes

Servings: 2

INGREDIENTS:

- 8 oz. package crimini or button mushrooms
- 2 garlic cloves, minced
- 2 tablespoon olive oil
- 1 tablespoon chopped thyme
- Salt and black pepper to taste

DIRECTIONS:

1. In a medium mixing bowl, combine the olive oil, garlic, and fresh thyme together. Whisk till well combined. Add pepper and salt to taste.
2. Pour the marinade on the mushrooms and mix well until the mushrooms are properly coated.
3. Place marinated mushrooms directly onto the lined pan.
4. Roast on the 'HI' setting for about 20 to 25 minutes.
5. Serve hot. Enjoy!

NUTRITION:

- Calories: 260
- Total Fat: 18g
- Carbs: 44g
- Protein: 6g

Sea Foods

Lemon Pepper Dill Fish

Preparation time: 5 minutes

Cooking time: 5 minutes

Serving: 4

INGREDIENTS:

- 1 pound haddock fillets
- 1/2 cup butter
- Dried dill weed to taste
- Lemon pepper to taste
- 3 tablespoons fresh lemon juice

DIRECTIONS:

1. Place fish fillets in a microwave-safe dish. Cut butter into pieces and place all over fish. Sprinkle with dill weed and lemon pepper. Drizzle fresh lemon juice all over the fish.

2. Cover and cook on high for 3 to 5 minutes or until the fish turns white.

NUTRITION:
- Calories: 305
- Total Fat: 23.8g
- Cholesterol: 125mg
- Sodium: 233mg
- Total Carbohydrate: 1g
- Protein: 21.7g

Healthy Fish and Chips

Preparation time: 5 minutes

Cooking time: 15 minutes

Servings: 3

INGREDIENTS:

- Old Bay seasoning
- 1/2 cup panko breadcrumbs
- 1 egg
- 2 tablespoon almond flour
- 4-6 ounce tilapia fillets
- Frozen crinkle cut fries

DIRECTIONS:

1. Add almond flour to one bowl, beat egg in another bowl, and add panko breadcrumbs to the third bowl, mixed with Old Bay seasoning.

2. Dredge tilapia in flour, then egg, and then breadcrumbs.

3. Place coated fish in the oven along with fries.

4. Set temperature to 390°F, and set time to 15 minutes.

NUTRITION:
- Calories: 219
- Fat: 5g
- Protein: 25g
- Sugar: 1g

Quick Paella

Preparation time: 7 minutes

Cooking time: 15 minutes

Servings: 4

INGREDIENTS:

- 1 (10-ounce) package frozen cooked rice, thawed
- 1 (6-ounce) jar artichoke hearts, drained and chopped
- 1/4 cup vegetable broth
- 1/2 teaspoon turmeric
- 1/2 teaspoon dried thyme
- 1 cup frozen cooked small shrimp
- 1/2 cup frozen baby peas
- 1 tomato, diced

DIRECTIONS:

1. In a 6-by-6-by-2-inch pan, combine the rice, artichoke hearts, vegetable broth, turmeric, and thyme, and stir gently.

2. Place in the oven and bake for 8 to 9 minutes or until the rice is hot. Remove from the oven and gently stir in the shrimp, peas, and tomato. Cook for 5 to 8 minutes or until the shrimp and peas are hot and the paella is bubbling.

NUTRITION:

- Calories: 345
- Fat: 1g
- Protein: 18g
- Fiber: 4g

Coconut Shrimp

Preparation time: 15 minutes

Cooking time: 5 minutes

Servings: 4

INGREDIENTS:

- 1 (8-ounce) can crushed pineapple
- 1/2 cup sour cream
- 1/4 cup pineapple preserves
- 2 egg whites
- 2/3 cup cornstarch
- 2/3 cup sweetened coconut
- 1 cup panko bread crumbs
- 1 pound uncooked large shrimp, thawed if frozen, deveined and shelled
- Olive oil for misting

DIRECTIONS:

1. Drain the crushed pineapple well, reserving the juice. In a small bowl, combine the pineapple, sour cream, and preserves, and mix well. Set aside. In a shallow bowl, beat the egg whites with 2 tablespoons of the reserved pineapple liquid. Place the cornstarch on a plate. Combine the coconut and bread crumbs on another plate. Dip the shrimp into the cornstarch, shake it off, then dip into the egg white mixture and finally into the coconut mixture. Place the shrimp in the oven basket and mist with oil.

2. Cook for 5 to 7 minutes or until the shrimp are crisp and golden brown

NUTRITION:
- Calories: 524
- Fat: 14g
- Protein: 33g
- Fiber: 4g

Ingredient Catfish

Preparation time: 5 minutes

Cooking time: 13 minutes

Servings: 4

INGREDIENTS:

- 1 tablespoon olive oil
- 1/4 cup seasoned fish fry
- 4 catfish fillets

DIRECTIONS:

1. Ensure your oven is preheated to 400 degrees.
2. Rinse off catfish fillets and pat dry.
3. Add fish fry seasoning to Ziploc baggie, then catfish. Shake bag and ensure fish gets well coated.
4. Spray each fillet with olive oil.
5. Add fillets to oven basket.
6. Set temperature to 400°F, and set time to 10 minutes.
7. Cook 10 minutes. Then flip and cook for another 2-3 minutes.

NUTRITION:

- Calories: 208
- Fat: 5g
- Protein: 17g
- Sugar: 0.5g

Cilantro-Lime Fried Shrimp

Preparation time: 10 minutes

Cooking time: 10 minutes

Servings: 4

INGREDIENTS:

- 1 pound raw shrimp, peeled and deveined with tails on or off (see Prep tip)
- 1/2 cup chopped fresh cilantro
- Juice of 1 lime
- 1 egg
- 1/2 cup all-purpose flour
- 3/4 cup bread crumbs
- Salt
- Pepper
- Cooking oil
- 1/2 cup cocktail sauce (optional)

DIRECTIONS:

1. Place the shrimp in a plastic bag and add the cilantro and lime juice. Seal the bag. Shake to combine. Marinate in the refrigerator for 30 minutes.

2. In a small bowl, beat the egg. In another small bowl, place the flour. Place the bread crumbs in a third small bowl, and season with salt and pepper to taste.

3. Spray the oven basket with cooking oil.

4. Remove the shrimp from the plastic bag. Dip each in the flour, the egg, and then the bread crumbs.

5. Place the shrimp in the oven. It is okay to stack them. Spray the shrimp with cooking oil. Cook for 4 minutes.

6. Open the oven and flip the shrimp. I recommend flipping individually instead of shaking to keep the breading intact. Cook for an additional 4 minutes, or until crisp.

7. Cool before serving. Serve with cocktail sauce if desired.

NUTRITION:
- Calories: 254
- Fat: 4g
- Protein: 29g
- Fiber: 1g

Bang Panko Breaded Fried Shrimp

Preparation time: 5 minutes

Cooking time: 8 minutes

Servings: 4

INGREDIENTS:

- 1 teaspoon paprika
- Montreal chicken seasoning
- 3/4 cup panko bread crumbs
- 1/2 cup almond flour
- 1 egg white
- 1 pound raw shrimp (peeled and deveined)

For Bang Bang Sauce:
- 1/4 cup sweet chili sauce
- 2 tablespoon sriracha sauce
- 1/3 cup plain Greek yogurt

DIRECTIONS:

1. Ensure your oven is preheated to 400 degrees.

2. Season all shrimp with seasonings.

3. Add flour to one bowl, egg white in another, and breadcrumbs to a third.

4. Dip seasoned shrimp in flour, then egg whites, and then breadcrumbs.

5. Spray coated shrimp with olive oil and add to oven basket.

6. Set temperature to 400°F, and set time to 4 minutes. Cook 4 minutes, flip, and cook an additional 4 minutes.

7. To make the sauce, mix together all sauce ingredients until smooth.

NUTRITION:

- Calories: 212
- Carbs: 12
- Fat: 1g
- Protein: 37g
- Sugar: 0.5g

Poultry

Korean Chicken Wings

Preparation time: 5 minutes

Cooking time: 10 minutes

Servings: 8

INGREDIENTS:

For the wings:
- 1 teaspoon pepper
- 1 teaspoon salt
- 2 pounds chicken wings

For the sauce:
- 2 packets Splenda
- 1 tablespoon minced garlic
- 1 tablespoon minced ginger
- 1 tablespoon sesame oil
- 1 teaspoon agave nectar
- 1 tablespoon mayo
- 2 tablespoon gochujang

Finishing:
- 1/4 cup chopped green onions
- 2 teaspoon sesame seeds

DIRECTIONS:

1. Ensure the oven is preheated to 400 degrees.
2. Line a small pan with foil and place a rack onto the pan, then place it into the oven.
3. Season wings with pepper and salt and place them onto the rack.
4. Set temperature to 160°F, and set time to 20 minutes and oven 20 minutes, turning at 10 minutes.
5. As chicken fries, mix together all the sauce components.
6. Once a thermometer says that the chicken has reached 160 degrees, take out wings and place them into a bowl.
7. Pour half of the sauce mixture over wings, tossing well to coat.
8. Put coated wings back into the oven for 5 minutes or till they reach 165 degrees.
9. Remove and sprinkle with green onions and sesame seeds. Dip into the extra sauce.

NUTRITION:

- Calories: 356
- Fat: 26g
- Protein: 23g
- Sugar: 2g

Almond Flour Coco-Milk Battered Chicken

Preparation time: 5 minutes

Cooking time: 30 minutes

Servings: 4

INGREDIENTS:

- 1/4 cup coconut milk
- 1/2 cup almond flour
- 1 1/2 tablespoons old bay Cajun seasoning
- 1 egg beaten
- 4 small chicken thighs
- Salt and pepper to taste

DIRECTIONS:

1. Preheat the oven for 5 minutes.
2. Mix the egg and coconut milk in a bowl.
3. Soak the chicken thighs in the beaten egg mixture.
4. In a mixing bowl, combine the almond flour, Cajun seasoning salt and pepper.
5. Dredge the chicken thighs in the almond flour mixture.
6. Place in the oven basket.
7. Cook for 30 minutes at 350°F.

NUTRITION:

- Calories: 590
- Fat: 38g
- Protein: 32.5g
- Carbs: 3.2g

Basil-Garlic Breaded Chicken Bake

Preparation time: 5 minutes

Cooking time: 25 minutes

Servings: 2

INGREDIENTS:

- 2 boneless skinless chicken breast halves (4 ounces each)
- 1 tablespoon butter, melted
- 1 large tomato, seeded and chopped
- 2 garlic cloves, minced
- 1 1/2 tablespoons minced fresh basil
- 1/2 tablespoon olive oil
- 1/2 teaspoon salt
- 1/4 cup all-purpose flour
- 1/4 cup egg substitute
- 1/4 cup grated Parmesan cheese
- 1/4 cup dry bread crumbs
- 1/4 teaspoon pepper

DIRECTIONS:

1. In a shallow bowl, whisk well egg substitute and place flour in a separate bowl. Dip chicken in flour, then egg, and then flour. In a small bowl whisk well butter, bread crumbs, and cheese. Sprinkle over chicken.

2. Lightly grease the baking pan of the oven with cooking spray. Place breaded chicken on the bottom of the pan. Cover with foil.

3. For 20 minutes, cook at 390°F.

4. Meanwhile, in a bowl, whisk well-remaining ingredients.

5. Remove foil from pan and then pour over chicken the remaining ingredients.

6. Cook for 8 minutes.

7. Serve and enjoy.

NUTRITION:

- Calories: 311
- Fat: 11g
- Protein: 31g
- Carbs: 22g

Buffalo Chicken Wings

Preparation time: 5 minutes

Cooking time: 30 minutes

Servings: 8

INGREDIENTS:

- 1 teaspoon salt
- 1-2 tablespoon brown sugar
- 1 tablespoon Worcestershire sauce
- 1/2 cup vegan butter
- 1/2 cup cayenne pepper sauce
- 4 pounds chicken wings

DIRECTIONS:

1. Whisk salt, brown sugar, Worcestershire sauce, butter, and hot sauce together and set to the side.

2. Dry wings and add to oven basket.

3. Set temperature to 380°F, and set time to 25 minutes. Cook tossing halfway through.

4. When the timer sounds, shake wings and bump up the temperature to 400 degrees and cook for another 5 minutes.

5. Take out wings and place them into a big bowl. Add sauce and toss well.

6. Serve alongside celery sticks.

NUTRITION:
- Calories: 402
- Fat: 16g
- Protein: 17g
- Sugar: 4g

Honey and Wine Chicken Breasts

Preparation time: 5 minutes

Cooking time: 15 minutes

Servings: 4

INGREDIENTS:

- 2 chicken breasts, rinsed and halved
- 1 tablespoon melted butter
- 1/2 teaspoon freshly ground pepper, or to taste
- 3/4 teaspoon sea salt, or to taste
- 1 teaspoon paprika
- 1 teaspoon dried rosemary
- 2 tablespoons dry white wine
- 1 tablespoon honey

DIRECTIONS:

1. Firstly, pat the chicken breasts dry. Lightly coat them with the melted butter.

2. Then, add the remaining ingredients.

3. Transfer them to the oven basket; bake for about 15 minutes at 330 degrees F. Serve warm and enjoy!

NUTRITION:
- Calories: 189
- Fat: 14g
- Protein: 11g
- Sugar: 1g

BBQ Chicken Recipe From Greece

Preparation time: 10 minutes

Cooking time: 25 minutes

Servings: 4

INGREDIENTS:

- 1 (8 ounces) container fat-free plain yogurt
- 2 tablespoons fresh lemon juice
- 2 teaspoons dried oregano
- 1-pound skinless, boneless chicken breast halves - cut into 1-inch pieces
- 1 large red onion, cut into wedges
- 1/2 teaspoon lemon zest
- 1/2 teaspoon salt
- 1 large green bell pepper, cut into 1 1/2-inch pieces
- 1/3 cup crumbled feta cheese with basil and sun-dried tomatoes
- 1/4 teaspoon ground black pepper
- 1/4 teaspoon crushed dried rosemary

DIRECTIONS:

1. In a shallow dish, mix well rosemary, pepper, salt, oregano, lemon juice, lemon zest, feta cheese, and yogurt. Add chicken and toss well to coat. Marinate in the ref for 3 hours.

2. Thread bell pepper, onion, and chicken pieces in skewers. Place on skewer rack.

3. For 12 minutes, cook at 360°F. Halfway through cooking time, turnover skewers. If needed, cook in batches.

4. Serve and enjoy.

NUTRITION:

- Calories: 242
- Fat: 7.5g
- Protein: 31g
- Sugar: 6g

Lemon-Pepper Chicken Wings

Preparation time: 10 minutes

Cooking time: 20 minutes

Servings: 4

INGREDIENTS:

- 8 whole chicken wings
- Juice of 1/2 lemon
- 1/2 teaspoon garlic powder
- 1 teaspoon onion powder
- Salt
- Pepper
- 1/4 cup low-fat buttermilk
- 1/2 cup all-purpose flour
- Cooking oil

DIRECTIONS:

1. Place the wings in a sealable plastic bag. Drizzle the wings with the lemon juice. Season the wings with garlic powder, onion powder, and salt and pepper to taste.//
2. Seal the bag. Shake thoroughly to combine the seasonings and coat the wings.
3. Pour the buttermilk and the flour into separate bowls large enough to dip the wings.
4. Spray the oven basket with cooking oil.
5. One at a time, dip the wings in the buttermilk and then the flour.
6. Place the wings in the oven basket. It is okay to stack them on top of each other. Spray the wings with cooking oil, being sure to spray the bottom layer. Cook for 5 minutes.
7. Remove the basket and shake it to ensure all of the pieces will cook fully.
8. Return the basket to the oven and continue to cook the chicken. Repeat shaking every 5 minutes until a total of 20 minutes has passed.
9. Cool before serving.

NUTRITION:

- Calories: 347
- Fat: 12g
- Protein: 46g
- Fiber: 1g

Caesar Marinated Grilled Chicken

Preparation time: 10 minutes

Cooking time: 24 minutes

Servings: 3

INGREDIENTS:

- 1/4 cup crouton
- 1 teaspoon lemon zest. Form into ovals, skewer, and grill.
- 1/2 cup Parmesan
- 1/4 cup breadcrumbs
- 1-pound ground chicken
- 2 tablespoons Caesar dressing and more for drizzling
- 2-4 romaine leaves

DIRECTIONS:

1. In a shallow dish, mix the chicken well, 2 tablespoons Caesar dressing, parmesan, and breadcrumbs. Mix well with hands. Form into 1-inch oval patties.

2. Thread chicken pieces in skewers. Place on skewer rack in oven.

3. For 12 minutes, cook at 360°F. Halfway through cooking time, turnover skewers. If needed, cook in batches.

4. Serve and enjoy on a bed of lettuce and sprinkle with croutons and extra dressing.

NUTRITION:
- Calories: 339
- Fat: 18.9g
- Protein: 32.6g
- Sugar: 1g

Crispy Southern Fried Chicken

Preparation time: 10 minutes

Cooking time: 25 minutes

Servings: 4

INGREDIENTS:

- 1 teaspoon cayenne pepper
- 2 tablespoon mustard powder
- 2 tablespoon oregano
- 2 tablespoon thyme
- 3 tablespoon coconut milk
- 1 beaten egg
- 1/4 cup cauliflower
- 1/4 cup gluten-free oats
- 8 chicken drumsticks

DIRECTIONS:

1. Ensure the oven is preheated to 350° F.
2. Prepare the chicken and season with pepper and salt on all sides.
3. Add all other ingredients to a blender, blending till a smooth-like breadcrumb mixture is created. Place in a bowl and add a beaten egg to another bowl.
4. Dip chicken into breadcrumbs, then into egg and breadcrumbs once more.
5. Place coated drumsticks into the oven basket. Set temperature to 350°F, and set time to 20 minutes and cook 20 minutes. Bump up the temperature to 390 degrees and cook another 5 minutes till crispy.

NUTRITION:
- Calories: 504
- Fat: 18g
- Protein: 35g
- Sugar: 5g

Meat

Steak With Garlic-Herb Butter

Preparation time: 15 minutes

Cooking time: 15 minutes

Servings: 2

INGREDIENTS:

- 1-pound sirloin steak, about 1-inch thick
- 1 teaspoon minced garlic
- 1/2 tablespoon salt
- 1/2 tablespoon ground black pepper
- 1 tablespoon chopped chives
- 1/4 teaspoon red pepper flakes
- 1 tablespoon chopped parsley
- 4 tablespoons butter, unsalted, softened

DIRECTIONS:

1. Turn on the oven, set the temperature to 400 degrees F, and then select the oven cooking method.
2. Meanwhile, prepare the steak and for this, season it with salt and black pepper.
3. Place the steak on the oven basket and then cook for 10 to 14 minutes until cooked to desire doneness.
4. When done, transfer the steak to a cutting board and then let it rest for 10 minutes.
5. In the meantime, place butter in a bowl, add garlic, chives, parsley, red bell flakes, and then stir until combined.
6. After 10 minutes, slice the steak into 1/4-inch thick pieces, top with the prepared garlic-herb mixture, and then serve.

NUTRITION:

- Calories: 409.8
- Fat: 30.8g
- Carbs: 3.1g

- Protein: 29.7g
- Fiber: 0.4g

Steak Bites With Mushrooms

Preparation time: 5 minutes

Cooking time: 18 minutes

Servings: 3

INGREDIENTS:

- 1-pound steak
- 8 ounces mushrooms, halved
- 1/2 teaspoon garlic powder
- 1 teaspoon salt
- 1/2 teaspoon ground black pepper
- 1 tablespoon minced parsley
- 2 tablespoons butter, unsalted, melted
- 1 teaspoon Worcestershire sauce

DIRECTIONS:

1. Turn on the oven, set the temperature to 400° F, and then select the oven cooking method.
2. Meanwhile, cut the steak into 1/2-inch cubes, rinse well and pat dry with paper towels.
3. Place the steak pieces in a bowl, add mushrooms, garlic powder, salt, and black pepper, drizzle with butter and Worcestershire sauce, and then toss until coated.
4. Spread the steak and mushroom pieces in a single layer on the oven basket and then cook for 18 minutes, tossing halfway through.
5. When done, garnish steaks and mushrooms with parsley and then serve.

NUTRITION:

- Calories: 401
- Fat: 29g
- Carbs: 3g
- Protein: 32g
- Fiber: 1g

Korean Beef BBQ

Preparation time: 5 minutes

Cooking time: 15 minutes

Servings: 4

INGREDIENTS:

- 1 pound steak, cut into thin slices
- 1/2 of a medium onion, peeled, cut into strips

For the marinade
- 1 tablespoon rice wine
- 1 tablespoon water
- 1 cup Korean BBQ sauce
- 2 tablespoons soy sauce

DIRECTIONS:

1. Take a large bowl, place onion and steak slices in it, and then add all the ingredients for the marinade.
2. Toss until coated and then marinate for a minimum of 6 hours in the refrigerator.
3. Turn on the oven, set the temperature to 350 degrees F, and then select the oven cooking method.
4. Meanwhile, take a baking pan, spread the steak and onion slices in a single layer, and then bake for 18 minutes.
5. Serve straight away.

NUTRITION:

- Calories: 334
- Fat: 21g
- Carbs: 12g
- Protein: 25g
- Fiber: 1g

Roast Beef

Preparation time: 10 minutes

Cooking time: 2 hours

Servings: 10

INGREDIENTS:

- 4 pounds round roast, fat trimmed
- 6 cloves of garlic, peeled, chopped

For the marinade:
- 1 teaspoon dried thyme
- 1 teaspoon salt
- 1 teaspoon ground black pepper
- 1 tablespoon chopped basil
- 1 tablespoon chopped rosemary
- 1/4 cup olive oil

DIRECTIONS:

1. Turn on the oven, set the temperature to 325 degrees F, and then select the oven cooking method.
2. Meanwhile, prepare the marinade and for this, place all of its ingredients in a small bowl and then stir until combined.
3. Make cuts into the roast, insert garlic slices in it, and then rub the marinade.
4. Place the prepared roast on the baking pan and then roast for 2 hours until done.
5. When done, let the roast rest for 15 minutes, cut it into slices, and then serve.

NUTRITION:

- Calories: 231
- Fat: 9g
- Carbs: 1g
- Protein: 36g
- Fiber: 1g

Bread

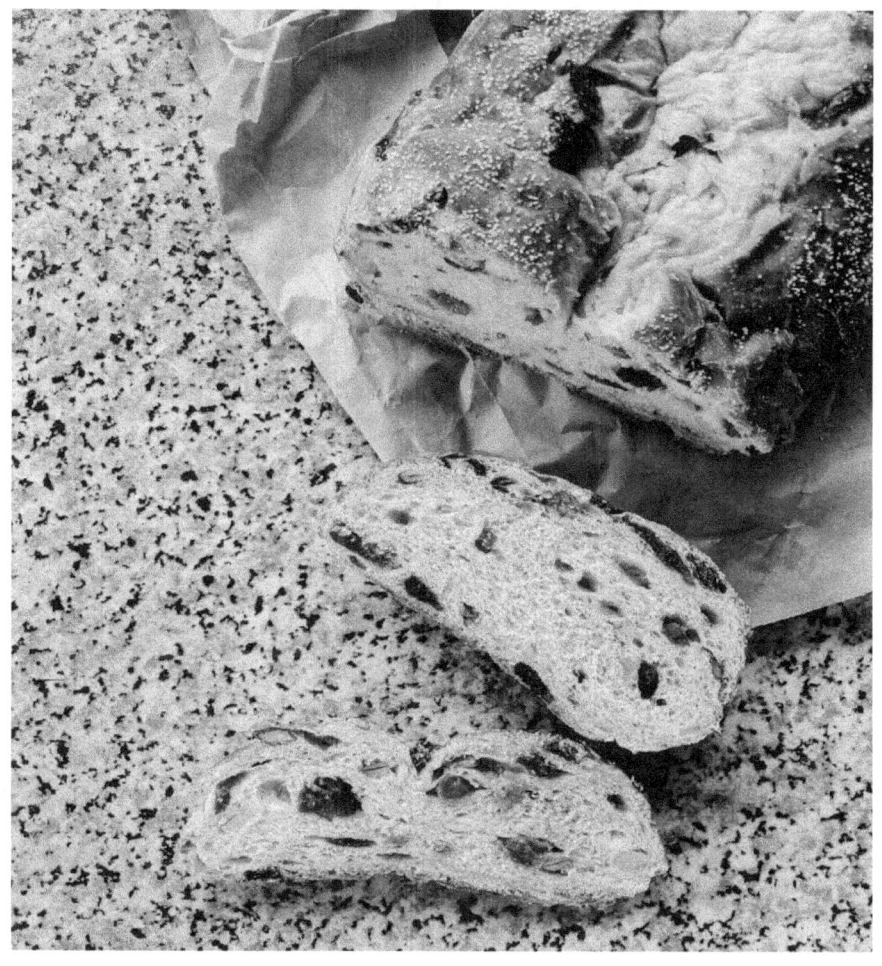

Cheddar Jalapeno Cornbread

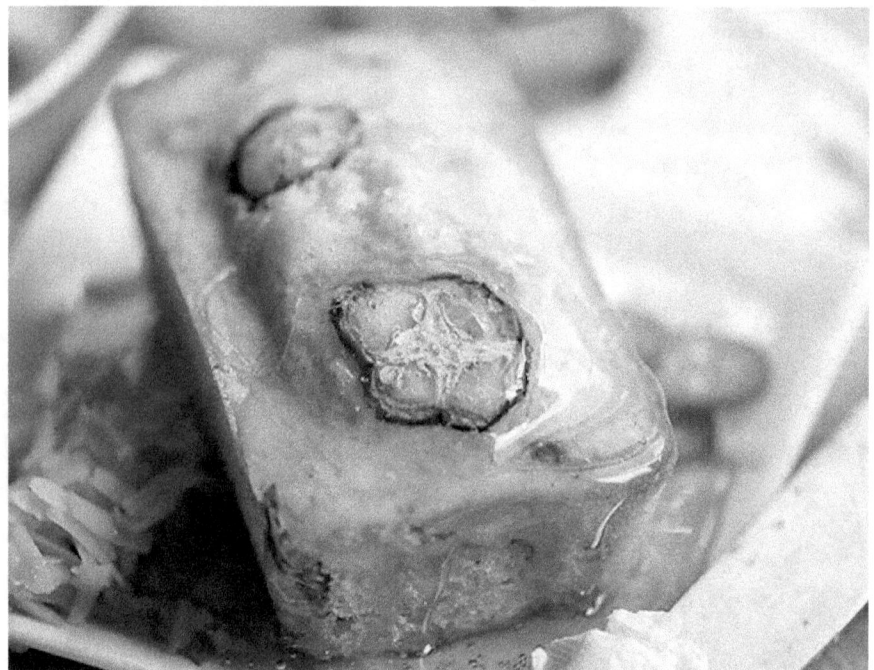

Preparation time: 20 minutes

Cooking time: 20 minutes

Servings: 6

INGREDIENTS:

- 1-1/2 cup all-purpose flour
- 1-1/2 cup yellow cornmeal
- 1-1/5 tablespoon baking powder
- 1-1/2 tablespoon salt
- 1-1/2 cup whole milk
- 1/4 tablespoon cayenne pepper, ground
- 3 eggs
- 1/2 cup sharp cheddar
- 1-1/2 tablespoon green jalapeno, minced
- 1-1/2 tablespoon red jalapeno, minced

- 1/3 cup vegetable oil plus 1 tablespoon vegetable oil
- 1-1/2 tablespoon honey
- 1/2 tablespoon butter

DIRECTIONS:

1. In a mixing bowl, mix flour, cornmeal, baking powder, salt, and pepper until well combined.
2. In another bowl, mix milk, eggs, cheese, jalapenos, and 1/3 cup vegetable oil.
3. Mix the dry ingredients into the wet ingredients. Grease a baking pan with the remaining oil and pour the mixture.
4. Slide the pizza rack on shelf position 5 of the Emeril Lagasse Power oven 360 and place the baking pan on top.
5. Select the bake setting. Set the temperature at 325°F for 30 minutes. Press start.
6. Cook until the toothpick comes out clean when inserted in the bread.
7. Brush the bread with honey and butter, then let rest to cool before serving.

NUTRITION:

- Calories: 201
- Carbs: 27g
- Fat: 8.2g
- Protein: 6g

Family Banana Nut Bread

Preparation time: 15 minutes

Cooking time: 1 hour

Servings: 10

INGREDIENTS:

- 8 oz. cream cheese, softened
- 1 cup white sugar
- 1/2 cup butter
- 2 eggs, beaten
- 2 ripe bananas, mashed

- 2-1/4 cups all-purpose flour
- 2 tablespoon baking soda
- 1-1/2 tablespoon baking powder
- 1 cup walnuts, chopped

DIRECTIONS:

1. Beat cream cheese, sugar, butter, eggs, and mashed banana in a mixing bowl until well mixed and smooth.
2. Stir with flour, baking soda, baking powder, and walnuts until well combined. Pour the batter on a greased loaf pan.
3. Slide the pizza rack on shelf position 5 and place the loaf pan on top.
4. Select the bake setting on the Emeril Lagasse Power oven 360 and set the temperature at 350°F for 75 minutes. Press start
5. Let the bread cool for 10 minutes before serving.

NUTRITION:

- Calories: 449
- Carbs: 49.3g
- Fat: 26g
- Protein: 8g

Basic Fruit Bread

Preparation time: 10 minutes

Cooking time: 40 minutes

Servings: 6

INGREDIENTS:

- 3 cups all-purpose flour
- 2 tablespoon baking powder
- 1 tablespoon baking soda
- 1/2 tablespoon salt
- 1 cup white sugar
- 1/2 cup vegetable oil
- 2 eggs
- 1 cup apple, shredded
- 3/4 cup walnuts, chopped
- 1/2 tablespoon vanilla extract

DIRECTIONS:

1. In a mixing bowl, mix flour, baking powder, baking soda, salt, white sugar, vegetable oil, eggs, apple, walnuts, and vanilla extract until moistened.
2. Grease the loaf pan and pour the mixture on it.
3. Slide the pizza rack on shelf position 5 of the Emeril Lagasse Power oven 360 and place the loaf pan on top.
4. Select the bake setting. Set the temperature at 350°F for 35 minutes. Press start.
5. Let the bread cool before serving.

NUTRITION:

- Calories: 391
- Carbs: 52g
- Fat: 18g
- Protein: 7g

Mini Pizza With Italian Sausage

Preparation time: 10 minutes

Cooking time: 30 minutes

Servings: 4

INGREDIENTS:

- 1 lb. pizza dough
- 1-1/2 lb. Hot Italian Sausage
- 3-1/2 tomato sauce
- 8 oz. mozzarella cheese
- 2 tablespoon thyme leaves, freshly chopped
- 1/2 tablespoon red pepper, crushed
- 1/4 cup Parmigiano-Reggiano, finely grated
- Extra virgin oil

DIRECTIONS:

1. Divide the dough into 4 portions on a work surface with flour. Roll each dough on the work surface into an 8 inches round.
2. Place the sausage on the crisper tray and slide the tray on position 2 of the Emeril Lagasse Power oven 360.
3. Select the oven setting and set the temperature at 400°F for 15 minutes. Press start.
4. Transfer the dough to the crisper tray and spoon the tomato sauce on each dough surface. Sprinkle cheese, top with the sausage, and garnish with thyme, pepper, and Parmigiano-Reggiano.
5. Slide the crisper tray on shelf position 2. Select the pizza setting. Set the temperature at 425°F for 20 minutes. Press start.
6. Repeat the cycle with the remaining 3 pizzas. Serve the pizza drizzled with olive oil.

NUTRITION:

- Calories: 130
- Carbs: 13g
- Fat: 5g
- Protein: 6g

Roasted Garlic Pizza With Garlic Sauce

Preparation time: 10 minutes

Cooking time: 30 minutes

Servings: 8

INGREDIENTS:

- 2 tablespoon butter, unsalted
- 2 tablespoon all-purpose flour
- 1 cup whole milk
- 1/4 tablespoon cayenne pepper, ground
- 3 heads garlic
- 1/4 tablespoon salt
- 1 cup of warm water
- 1 tablespoon honey
- 2 tablespoon olive oil
- 1-1/4 oz. active dry yeast
- 2-1/2 cup all-purpose flour
- 8 oz. mozzarella cheese
- 4 oz. fontina cheese, grated
- 1/2 cup Parmigiano-Reggiano cheese, finely grated
- 30 pieces tomatoes, sun-dried

- 2 tablespoon basil leaves, freshly chopped
- 1 tablespoon chopped parsley

DIRECTIONS:

1. Melt butter in a saucepan over medium heat and cook the all-purpose flour for 3 minutes.
2. Whisk in milk until thickened. Add pepper, garlic, and salt, then simmer for 15 minutes on low heat to make the bechamel.
3. In a mixing bowl, mix warm water honey, and oil. Mix in the yeast, flour, and salt to the bowl. Knead until smooth. Let rest for 20 minutes.
4. Divide the pizza dough into half and roll it to make it fit the pizza rack.
5. Top with cheeses and tomatoes. Slide the pizza rack on position 5 and select the pizza setting on the Emeril Lagasse Power oven 360.
6. Set the temperature at 425°F for 20 minutes. Press start.
7. Repeat with the second pizza. Top the pizza with parsley, basil, and red pepper.

NUTRITION:

- Calories: 280
- Carbs: 34g
- Fat: 11g
- Protein: 12g

Cake & Dessert

Cinnamon Apple Tart

Preparation time: 10 minutes

Cooking time: 15 minutes

Servings: 1

INGREDIENTS:

- 2 teaspoons light brown sugar
- 1/2 teaspoon ground cinnamon
- 1 (6-inch) flour tortilla
- 1 tablespoon unsalted butter
- 1/2 honey crisp apple
- Salt to taste

DIRECTIONS:

1. Melt butter and slice apples into 1/8-inch-thick slices.
2. Mix together cinnamon and sugar.
3. Brush tortilla with butter and sprinkle with half the sugar and cinnamon.

4. Toast in toaster oven until tortilla crisps, about 3 minutes.
5. Arrange the apple slices in a circle around the tortilla.
6. Return to toaster oven and toast for another 10 minutes.
7. Sprinkle with salt to taste.

NUTRITION:

- Calories: 227
- Sodium: 250mg
- Dietary Fiber: 4.3g
- Total Fat: 12.4g
- Total Carbs: 30.1g
- Protein: 1.8g

Blackberry Peach Cobbler

Preparation time: 25 minutes

Cooking time: 30 minutes

Servings: 12

INGREDIENTS:

- 1-1/2 cups sliced peaches
- 1 cup blackberries
- 3 tablespoons coconut sugar
- 1-1/2 teaspoons cinnamon
- 2-1/2 cups dry oats
- 1 egg
- 1/2 cup unsweetened applesauce
- 3/4 cup almond milk
- 1/2 cup chopped walnuts
- 1 tablespoon coconut oil, melted
- 1/2 teaspoon cinnamon

DIRECTIONS:

1. Start by preheating the toaster oven to 350°F.
2. Combine peaches, berries, sugar, and 1 teaspoon cinnamon in a medium saucepan over medium heat. Simmer for about 20 minutes, stirring regularly.
3. While peach mixture cooks, beat egg in a large bowl, then mix in applesauce and milk.
4. In a separate bowl, add egg mixture to the oats.
5. Pour oats mixture into a greased baking pan and top with peach mixture.
6. Combine coconut oil, walnuts, coconut sugar, and 1/2 teaspoon cinnamon, and pour over pan.
7. Bake for 30 minutes

NUTRITION:

- Calories: 176
- Sodium: 9mg
- Dietary Fiber: 3.7g
- Total Fat: 9.4g
- Total Carbs: 20.6g
- Protein: 4.7g.

Blueberry Cream Cheese Croissant Puff

Preparation time: 30 minutes

Cooking time: 40 minutes

Servings: 10

INGREDIENTS:

- 3 large croissants
- 1 cup fresh or frozen blueberries
- 1 package (8-ounce) cream cheese
- 2/3 cup sugar
- 2 eggs
- 1 teaspoon vanilla
- 1 cup milk

DIRECTIONS:

1. Start by preheating toaster oven to 350°F.
2. Tear up croissants into 2-inch chunks and place in a square pan.
3. Sprinkle blueberries over croissant chunks.
4. In a medium bowl, combine cream cheese, sugar, eggs, and vanilla.
5. Slowly add milk, mixing as you add.
6. Pour cream cheese mixture over croissants and let stand for 20 minutes.
7. Bake for 40 minutes.

NUTRITION:

- Calories: 140
- Sodium: 97mg
- Dietary Fiber: 0.5g
- Total Fat: 5.8g
- Total Carbs: 20.0g
- Protein: 3.2g.

Oatmeal Cookie Peach Cobbler

Preparation time: 40 minutes

Cooking time: 40 minutes

Servings: 12

INGREDIENTS:

Topping
- 1/2 cup granulated sugar
- 1/2 cup packed brown sugar
- 1/2 cup softened butter
- 2 teaspoons vanilla extract
- 1 large egg
- 1 cup all-purpose flour
- 1 cup old-fashioned rolled oats
- 1/2 teaspoon baking powder
- 1/2 teaspoon salt

Filling
- 11 cups sliced peeled peaches
- 1/3 cup granulated sugar
- 2 tablespoons all-purpose flour
- 2 tablespoons fresh lemon juice

DIRECTIONS:

1. Start by preheating toaster oven to 350°F.
2. Combine butter and sugars in a medium bowl until creamed and set aside.
3. Add vanilla and egg and mix well.
4. Combine flour, oats, and baking powder in a separate bowl.
5. Mix sugar mixture and flour mixture together.
6. Cover the bowl and refrigerate for half an hour.
7. While topping chills, make the filling by combining peaches, lemon juice, flour, and sugar in a bowl.
8. Spray a baking dish with cooking spray and fill with peach mix.
9. Dollop spoonfuls of topping evenly over peaches. Bake for 40 minutes.

NUTRITION:

- Calories: 281
- Sodium: 160mg
- Dietary Fiber: 3.4g
- Total Fat: 9.0g
- Total Carbs: 48.5g
- Protein: 4.2g.

Oatmeal Raisin Cookies

Preparation time: 10 minutes

Cooking time: 20 minutes

Servings: 12

INGREDIENTS:

- 2-1/2 cups uncooked oatmeal
- 1 cup flour
- 2 eggs
- 1/2 teaspoon salt
- 1 cup butter
- 1 teaspoon vanilla
- 1 cup brown sugar
- 1/3 cup sugar
- 1 teaspoon baking soda
- 1 teaspoon ground cinnamon

- 1 cup raisins

DIRECTIONS:

1. Start by preheating the toaster oven to 350°F.
2. Mix together vanilla, brown sugar, butter, and salt.
3. Add flour, sugar, eggs, baking soda, and cinnamon one at a time until fully mixed.
4. Stir in the oats, then the raisins.
5. Drop spoonfuls of cookie dough onto an ungreased baking sheet (about six per batch).
6. Bake for 20 minutes.

NUTRITION:

- **Calories:** 353
- **Sodium:** 326mg
- **Dietary Fiber:** 2.6g
- **Total Fat:** 17.3g
- **Total Carbs:** 46.7g
- **Protein:** 4.8g.

Peanut Butter and Jelly Bars

Preparation time: 10 minutes

Cooking time: 20 minutes

Servings: 8

INGREDIENTS:

- 1/2 cup whole wheat pastry flour
- 1/2 teaspoon baking powder
- 1/4 teaspoon salt
- 1 small banana
- 1/4 cup smooth peanut butter
- 3 tablespoons real maple syrup
- 2 teaspoons melted coconut oil
- 1/2 teaspoon pure vanilla extract
- 2 tablespoons chopped raw shelled peanuts
- 2 tablespoons raspberry preserves

DIRECTIONS:

1. Start by preheating the toaster oven to 350°F.
2. Mash the banana.

3. Mix banana, syrup, oil, peanut butter, and vanilla in a bowl until thoroughly combined.
4. In a separate large bowl add flour, salt, and baking powder and combine using a fork.
5. Create a hole in the flour mix and pour in the banana mix.
6. Sprinkle with nuts and stir for 2 minutes.
7. Pour batter into a bread loaf pan lined with parchment paper. Drop 1/2 teaspoonful of raspberry preserves over batter.
8. Bake for 20 minutes.
9. Allow to cool, then transfer using the parchment paper and cut.

NUTRITION:

- Calories: 143
- Sodium: 78mg
- Dietary Fiber: 1.8g
- Total Fat: 6.5g
- Total Carbs: 19.0g
- Protein: 3.5g.

Peanut Butter Cookies

Preparation time: 10 minutes

Cooking time: 10 minutes

Servings: 1

INGREDIENTS:

- 2 tablespoons flour
- 1-1/2 tablespoons peanut butter
- 1/16 teaspoon baking soda
- Pinch of salt
- 1/4 teaspoon pure vanilla extract
- 1-1/2 tablespoons maple syrup
- 1 teaspoon applesauce

DIRECTIONS:

1. Start by preheating the toaster oven to 350°F.

2. Mix all of the dry ingredients together in one bowl.
3. Mix in peanut butter, then the rest of the ingredients.
4. Spray a small pan and drop cookies onto the pan, then flatten.
5. Bake for 10 minutes.

NUTRITION:

- Calories: 281
- Sodium: 348mg
- Dietary Fiber: 1.9g
- Total Fat: 12.3g
- Total Carbs: 37.5g
- Protein: 7.6g.

Cinnamon Pear Oatmeal Crisp

Preparation time: 10 minutes

Cooking time: 25 minutes

Servings: 1

INGREDIENTS:

- 1 cup pears, peeled and thinly sliced
- 2 tablespoons rolled oats
- 1 tablespoon whole wheat pastry flour
- 1 tablespoon brown sugar
- 1 tablespoon butter
- 1/2 teaspoon cinnamon
- Freshly grated nutmeg to taste

DIRECTIONS:

1. Preheat toaster oven to 375°F.
2. Place pears in an oven-safe dish.
3. In a separate bowl, mix together all other ingredients and pour on top of pears.
4. Bake for 25 minutes.

NUTRITION:

- Calories: 300
- Sodium: 87mg
- Dietary Fiber: 7.4g
- Total Fat: 12.7g
- Total Carbs: 46.9g
- Protein: 2.9g

Measurement Conversion Chart

		American and British Variances			
Term	Abbreviation	Nationality	Dry or liquid	Metric equivalent	Equivalent in context
cup	c., C.		usually liquid	237 milliliters	16 tablespoons or 8 ounces
ounce	fl oz, fl. oz.	American	liquid only	29.57 milliliters	
		British	either	28.41 milliliters	
gallon	gal.	American	liquid only	3.785 liters	4 quarts
		British	either	4.546 liters	4 quarts
inch	in, in.			2.54 centimeters	
ounce	oz, oz.	American	dry	28.35 grams	1/16 pound
			liquid	see OUNCE	see OUNCE
pint	p., pt.	American	liquid	0.473 liter	1/8 gallon or 16 ounces
			dry	0.551 liter	1/2 quart
		British	either	0.568 liter	
pound	lb.		dry	453.592 grams	16 ounces
Quart	q., qt, qt.	American	liquid	0.946 liter	1/4 gallon or 32 ounces
			dry	1.101 liters	2 pints
		British	either	1.136 liters	
Teaspoon	t., tsp., tsp		either	about 5 milliliters	1/3 tablespoon
Tablespoon	T., tbs., tbsp.		either	about 15 milliliters	3 teaspoons or 1/2 ounce

Volume (Liquid)

American Standard (Cups & Quarts)	American Standard (Ounces)	Metric (Milliliters & Liters)
2 tbsp.	1 fl. oz.	30 ml
1/4 cup	2 fl. oz.	60 ml
1/2 cup	4 fl. oz.	125 ml
1 cup	8 fl. oz.	250 ml
1 1/2 cups	12 fl. oz.	375 ml
2 cups or 1 pint	16 fl. oz.	500 ml
4 cups or 1 quart	32 fl. oz.	1000 ml or 1 liter
1 gallon	128 fl. oz.	4 liters

Volume (Dry)

American Standard	Metric
1/8 teaspoon	5 ml
1/4 teaspoon	1 ml
1/2 teaspoon	2 ml
3/4 teaspoon	4 ml
1 teaspoon	5 ml
1 tablespoon	15 ml
1/4 cup	59 ml
1/3 cup	79 ml
1/2 cup	118 ml
2/3 cup	158 ml
3/4 cup	177 ml
1 cup	225 ml
2 cups or 1 pint	450 ml
3 cups	675 ml
4 cups or 1 quart	1 liter
1/2 gallon	2 liters
1 gallon	4 liters

Dry Measure Equivalents

3 teaspoons	1 tablespoon	1/2 ounce	14.3 grams
2 tablespoons	1/8 cup	1 ounce	28.3 grams
4 tablespoons	1/4 cup	2 ounces	56.7 grams
5 1/3 tablespoons	1/3 cup	2.6 ounces	75.6 grams
8 tablespoons	1/2 cup	4 ounces	113.4 grams
12 tablespoons	3/4 cup	6 ounces	.375 pound
32 tablespoons	2 cups	16 ounces	1 pound

Oven Temperatures

American Standard	Metric
250° F	130° C
300° F	150° C
350° F	180° C
400° F	200° C
450° F	230° C

Weight (Mass)

American Standard (Ounces)	Metric (Grams)
1/2 ounce	15 grams
1 ounce	30 grams
3 ounces	85 grams
3.75 ounces	100 grams
4 ounces	115 grams
8 ounces	225 grams
12 ounces	340 grams
16 ounces or 1 pound	450 grams

www.ingramcontent.com/pod-product-compliance
Lightning Source LLC
Chambersburg PA
CBHW070925080526
44589CB00013B/1431